IN NATURE'S HEART

The Wilderness Days of
John Muir

Selections from Muir's Writings

with

Photographs by James Randklev

A Walking Stick Press Book

The Nature Company Classics

The Nature Company owes its vision to the world's great naturalists: Charles Darwin, Henry David Thoreau, John Muir, David Brower, Rachel Carson, Jacques Cousteau, and many others. Through their inspiration, we are dedicated to providing products and experiences which encourage the joyous observation, understanding, and appreciation of nature. We do not advocate, and will not allow to be sold in our stores, any products which result from the killing of wild animals for trophy purposes. Seashells, butterflies, furs, and mounted animal specimens fall into this category. Our goal is to provide you with products, insights, and experiences which kindle your own sense of wonder and which help you to feel good about yourself and the world in which you live.

In Nature's Heart was prepared for publication at Walking Stick Press, San Francisco
  Designed by Linda Herman
  Edited by Diana Landau

The Nature Company staff:
Priscilla Wrubel, Ed Strobin, Steve Manning, Georganne Papac, Tracy Fortini

Typesetting by Wilsted & Taylor
Produced by Mandarin Offset
Printed and bound in Hong Kong

Sixth Printing

CONTENTS

PREFACE

*"One can make a day of any size, and regulate the rising
and setting of his own sun and the brightness of its shining."*

John Muir was never happier than when rambling about alone in
wild country. Though he is best remembered as America's foremost
conservationist and the heroic leader of early wilderness preservation
battles, he often protested that "this formal, legal, unwild work is out
of my line." He faithfully performed such work until his death in
1914 but never forgot why he was doing it, or lost the sense of wonder and delight that flowered during his famous "first summer" in
the Sierra, as a young man in 1869.

Muir's passionate interest in wild nature was explored and ex-
pressed in many ways. He had a keen scientific curiosity, and
pursued a serious study of glaciers in the Sierra Nevada and Alaska
that helped advance geological knowledge. Like any dedicated natu-
ralist, he made copious sketches and notes from his observations of
flora and fauna. As a literary artist, he found aesthetic pleasure and
inspiration in wilderness; as a spiritual seeker, he glimpsed the Crea-
tor through "a thousand windows" of primeval creation.

But it was perhaps on the most personal level that nature spoke
to him most eloquently. Muir hadn't much of a childhood: raised in a
poor village in Scotland and on a Wisconsin farm, he was tyrannized
by a father who demanded a man's ration of hard labor from his son
and punished any boyish larking about in the woods. John lit out for
the territories as soon as he finished college and kept going until he
reached the Sierra Nevada. On that first pilgrimage to the mountains, he found his freedom, his vocation, his mission, his religion,

his true home, and a nurturing, bountiful parent. And he rediscovered the child in himself, who could experience unfettered joy and an easeful harmony with his surroundings. A note of pure childlike delight is present in all his nature writing after that time.

In Muir's books are many accounts of entire memorable days he spent in the wild—days framed by the sun's rising and setting—and we have framed this book in the same way. Typically, Muir would spring up from his bed of boughs at first light and set off after a breakfast of tea and bread, with just a crust fastened to his belt for lunch. Often he had a specific destination—a mountain peak, glacier, or distant meadow—sometimes not. Wild weather was an excuse to get out and revel in nature's forces; Muir's eagerness to get "close to the heart of the world" led him into close encounters with bears, storms, earthquakes, and other adventures that we might call hardships. By day's end his energy had flagged not a whit: "When night was drawing near, I ran down the flowery slopes exhilarated. . . . all the world seemed new-born."

Muir's enthusiasm for "our grand wildernesses" was inexhaustible, and fortunately for us all, he was compelled to share it, "calling everybody to come and enjoy the thousand blessings they have to offer." His writing has awakened in countless readers the desire to live in the freedom of a wilderness day, and the determination to preserve such opportunities for generations to come. We hope this selection of Muir's words will inspire more readers to "climb the mountains and get their good tidings"—and to visit his books as well.

D A W N

atching the daybreak and sunrise. The pale rose and purple sky changing softly to daffodil yellow and white, sunbeams pouring through the passes between the peaks and over the Yosemite domes, making their edges burn; the silver firs in the middle ground catching the glow on their spiry tops, and our camp grove fills and thrills with the glorious light. Everything awakening and joyful; the birds begin to stir and innumerable insect people. Deer quietly withdraw into leafy hiding-places in the chaparral; the dew vanishes, flowers spread their petals, every pulse beats high, every life cell rejoices, the very rocks seem to thrill with life. The whole landscape glows like a human face in a glory of enthusiasm, and the blue sky, pale around the horizon, bends peacefully down over all like one vast flower.

HOW GLORIOUS A greeting the sun gives the mountains! To behold this alone is worth the pains of any excursion a thousand times over. The highest peaks burned like islands in a sea of liquid shade. Then the lower peaks and spires caught the glow, and long lances of light, streaming through many a notch and pass, fell thick upon the frozen meadows.

I SPRING TO my feet crying: "Heavens and earth! Rock is not light, not heavy, not transparent, not opaque, but every pore gushes, glows like a thought with immortal life!"

FRESH BEAUTY OPENS one's eyes wherever it is really seen, but the very abundance and completeness of the common beauty that besets our steps prevents its being absorbed and appreciated. It is a good thing, therefore, to make short excursions now and then to the bottom of the sea among dulse and coral, or up among the clouds on mountain-tops, or in balloons, or even to creep like worms into dark holes and caverns underground, not only to learn something of what is going on in those out-of-the-way places, but to see better what the sun sees on our return to common everyday beauty.

HOW DEATHLIKE IS sleep in this mountain air, and quick the awakening into newness of life!

THE LAST DAYS of this glacial winter are not yet past, so young is our world. I used to envy the father of our race, dwelling as he did in contact with the new-made fields and plants of Eden; but I do so no more, because I have discovered that I also live in "creation's dawn." The morning stars still sing together, and the world, not yet half made, becomes more beautiful every day.

THE FORESTS . . . seem kindly familiar, and the lakes and meadows and glad singing streams. I should like to dwell with them forever. Here with bread and water I should be content. . . . Bathed in such beauty, watching the expressions ever varying on the faces of the mountains, watching the stars, which here have a glory that the lowlander never dreams of, watching the circling seasons, listening to the songs of the waters and winds and birds, would be endless pleasure. And what glorious cloudlands I should see, storms and calms—a new heaven and a new earth every day. . . .

M O R N I N G

Fine calm morning; air tense and clear; not the slightest breeze astir; everything shining, the rocks with wet crystals, the plants with dew, each receiving its portion of irised dewdrops and sunshine like living creatures getting their breakfast, their dew manna coming down from the starry sky like swarms of smaller stars. How wondrous fine are the particles in showers of dew, thousands required for a single drop, growing in the dark as silently as the grass! What pains are taken to keep this wilderness in health—showers of snow, showers of rain, showers of dew, floods of light, floods of invisible vapor, clouds, winds, all sorts of weather. . . . How fine Nature's methods! How deeply with beauty is beauty overlaid!

LONG BEFORE I had traced this fine stream [Yosemite Creek] to its head . . . I was eager to reach the extreme verge to see how it behaved in flying so far through the air; but after enjoying this view and getting safely away I have never advised any one to follow my steps. The last incline down which the stream journeys so gracefully is so steep and smooth one must slip cautiously forward on hands and feet alongside the rushing water. . . . But to gain a perfect view one must go yet farther, over a curving brow to a slight shelf on the extreme brink. . . . Noticing some tufts of artemisia in a cleft of rock, I filled my mouth with the leaves, hoping their bitter taste might help to keep caution keen and prevent giddiness. In spite of myself I reached the little ledge, got my heels well set, and worked sidewise twenty or thirty feet to a point close to the out-plunging current. Here the view is perfectly free down into the heart of the bright irised throng of comet-like streamers into which the whole ponderous volume of the fall separates. . . . So glorious a display of pure wildness . . . is terribly impressive.

LOOKING EASTWARD FROM the summit of Pacheco Pass one shining morning, a landscape was displayed that after all my wanderings still appears as the most beautiful I have ever beheld. At my feet lay the Great Central Valley of California, level and flowery, like a lake of pure sunshine, forty or fifty miles wide, five hundred miles long, one rich furred garden of yellow Compositae. And from the eastern boundary of this vast golden flower-bed rose the mighty Sierra, miles in height, and so gloriously colored and so radiant, it seemed not clothed with light but wholly composed of it, like the wall of some celestial city. . . . Then it seemed to me that the Sierra should be called, not the Nevada or Snowy Range, but the Range of Light. And after ten years of wandering and wondering in the heart of it, rejoicing in its glorious floods of light, the white beams of the morning streaming through the passes, the noonday radiance on the crystal rocks, the flush of the alpenglow, and the irised spray of countless waterfalls, it still seems above all others the Range of Light.

IT WAS RAINING hard when I awoke, but I made up my mind to disregard the weather . . . and with my indispensable ice-axe plunged once more into the dripping jungle. . . . The smell of the washed ground and vegetation made every breath a pleasure, and I found *Calypso borealis*, the first I had seen on this side of the continent, one of my darlings, worth any amount of hardship; and I saw one of my Douglas squirrels on the margin of a grassy pool. . . . The mosses were indescribably beautiful, so fresh, so bright, so cheerily green, and all so low and calm and silent, however heavy and wild the wind and the rain blowing and pouring above them. Surely never a particle of dust has touched leaf or crown of all these blessed mosses. . . . And the wet berries, Nature's precious jewelry, how beautiful they were! and the glittering, berry-like raindrops adorning the interlacing arches of bent grasses and sedges around the edges of the pools, every drop a mirror with all the landscape in it.

. . . In the gardens and forests of this wonderful moraine one might spend a whole joyful life.

MOST DELIGHTFUL IT is to stand in the middle of Yosemite on still clear mornings after snow-storms and watch the throng of avalanches as they come down, rejoicing, to their places, whispering, thrilling like birds, or booming and roaring like thunder. The noble yellow pines stand hushed and motionless as if under a spell until the morning sunshine begins to sift through their laden spires; then the dense masses on the ends of the leafy branches begin to shift and fall . . . enveloping each tree in a hollow conical avalanche of fairy fineness; while the relieved branches spring up and wave with startling effect in the general stillness, as if each tree was moving of its own volition.

SO EXTRAVAGANT IS Nature with her choicest treasures, spending plant beauty as she spends sunshine, pouring it forth into land and sea, garden and desert. And so the beauty of lilies falls on angels and men, bears and squirrels, wolves and sheep, birds and bees. . . .

THE WINDS WANDER, the snow and rain and dew fall, the earth whirls—all but to prosper a poor lush violet.

SURELY ALL GOD's people, however serious or savage, great or small, like to play. Whales and elephants, dancing, humming gnats, and invisibly small mischievous microbes—all are warm with divine radium and must have lots of fun in them.

NO SIERRA LANDSCAPE that I have seen holds anything truly dead or dull . . . everything is perfectly clean and pure and full of divine lessons. This quick, inevitable interest attaching to everything seems marvelous until the hand of God becomes visible; then it seems reasonable that what interests Him may well interest us. When we try to pick out anything by itself, we find it hitched to everything else in the universe. One fancies a heart like our own must be beating in every crystal and cell. . . .

M I D D A Y

umuli rising to the eastward. How beautiful their pearly bosses! How well they harmonize with the upswelling rocks beneath them. Mountains of the sky, solid-looking, finely sculptured, their richly varied topography wonderfully defined. Never before have I seen clouds so substantial looking in form and texture. Nearly every day toward noon they rise with visible swelling motion as if new worlds were being created. . . . What can poor mortals say about clouds?

ANOTHER GLORIOUS SIERRA day in which one seems to be dissolved and absorbed and sent pulsing onward we know not where. Life seems neither long nor short, and we take no more heed to save time or make haste than do the trees and stars. This is true freedom, a good practical sort of immortality.

ONE OF THE most beautiful and exhilarating storms I ever enjoyed in the Sierra occurred in December, 1874. The day was intensely pure, one of those incomparable bits of California winter, warm and balmy and full of white sparkling sunshine, and at the same time enlivened with one of the most bracing wind-storms conceivable. . . . I lost no time in pushing out into the woods to enjoy it.

 . . . Toward midday . . . I gained the summit of the highest ridge in the neighborhood; and then it occurred to me that it would be a fine thing to climb one of the trees to obtain a wider outlook and get my ear close to the Aeolian music of its topmost needles. . . . After cautiously casting about I made choice of the tallest of a group of Douglas Spruces. . . . they were about 100 feet high, and their lithe, brushy tops were rocking and swirling in wild ecstasy. Being accustomed to climb trees in making botanical studies, I experienced no difficulty in reaching the top of this one, and never before did I enjoy so noble an exhilaration of motion. The slender tops fairly flapped and swished in the passionate torrent . . . round and round, tracing indescribable combinations of vertical and horizontal curves, while I clung with muscles firm braced, like a bobolink on a reed. . . . I kept my lofty perch for hours, frequently closing my eyes to enjoy the music by itself, or to feast quietly on the fragrance that was streaming past.

. . . We all travel the milky way together, trees and men; but it never occurred to me until this storm-day, while swinging in the wind, that trees are travelers, in the ordinary sense. They make many journeys, not extensive ones, it is true; but our own little journeys, away and back again, are only little more than tree-wavings—many of them not so much.

I NEVER SAW a discontented tree. They grip the ground as though they liked it, and though fast rooted they travel about as far as we do.

ABOUT NOON, WHEN the tide was in our favor, we set out on the return trip to the gold-mine camp. The sun shone free and warm. No wind stirred. The water spaces between the bergs were as smooth as glass, reflecting the unclouded sky, and doubling the ravishing beauty of the bergs as the sunlight streamed through their innumerable angles in rainbow colors. . . .

On days like this, true sun-days, some of the bergs show a purplish tinge, though most are white from the disintegrating of their weathered surfaces. Now and then a new-born one is met that is pure blue crystal throughout, freshly broken from the fountain or recently exposed to the air by turning over. But in all of them, old and new, there are azure caves and rifts of ineffable beauty, in which the purest tones of light pulse and shimmer, lovely and untainted as anything on earth or in the sky.

MAKING YOUR WAY through the fertile wilderness . . . you suddenly emerge from the forest shadows upon a delightful purple lawn lying smooth and free in the light like a lake. This is a glacier meadow. . . . With inexpressible delight you wade out into the grassy sun-lake, feeling yourself contained in one of Nature's most sacred chambers, withdrawn from the sterner influences of the mountains, secure from all intrusion, secure from yourself, free in the universal beauty. And notwithstanding the scene is so impressively spiritual, and you seem dissolved in it, yet everything about you is beating with warm, terrestrial, human love and life. . . . You are all eye, sifted through and through with light and beauty.

BY FORCES SEEMINGLY antagonistic and destructive Nature accomplishes her beneficent designs—now a flood of fire, now a flood of ice, now a flood of water; and again in the fullness of time an outburst of organic life. . . .

NOTHING GOES UNRECORDED. Every word of leaf and snow-flake and particle of dew . . . as well as earthquake and avalanche, is written down in Nature's book.

AFTERNOON

fter luncheon I made haste to high ground, and from the top of the ridge on the west side of Indian Cañon gained the noblest view of the summit peaks I have ever yet enjoyed. Nearly the entire upper basin of the Merced was displayed, with its sublime domes and cañons, dark upsweeping forests, and glorious array of white peaks deep in the sky, every feature glowing, radiating beauty that pours into our flesh and bones like heat rays from fire. Sunshine over all; no breath of wind to stir the brooding calm. Never before had I seen so glorious a land-scape, so boundless an affluence of sublime mountain beauty.

OH, THESE VAST, calm, measureless mountain days, inciting at once to work and rest! Days in whose light everything seems equally divine, opening a thousand windows to show us God. Nevermore, however weary, should one faint by the way who gains the blessing of one mountain day; whatever his fate, long life, short life, stormy or calm, he is rich forever.

THE WARM, BROODING days are full of life and thoughts of life to come, ripening seeds with next summer in them or a hundred summers.

MOUNT RITTER IS king of the mountains of the middle portion of the High Sierra. . . . as far as I know it had never been climbed. Its height above sea-level is about 13,300 feet and it is fenced round by steeply inclined glaciers and cañons of tremendous depth and ruggedness, which render it almost inaccessible. But difficulties of this kind only exhilarate the mountaineer.

[The day of the ascent] Everything encouraged my undertaking and betokened success. There was no cloud in the sky, no storm-tone in the wind. I fastened a hard, durable crust to my belt by way of provision, in case I should be compelled to pass a night on the mountain-top; then . . . set forth free and hopeful.

I succeeded in gaining the foot of the cliff on the eastern extremity of the glacier . . . [and] thus made my way into a wilderness of crumbling spires and battlements, built together in bewildering combinations, and glazed in many places with a thin coating of ice, which I had to hammer off with stones. The situation was becoming gradually more perilous; but . . . I dared not think of descending; for, so steep was the entire ascent, one would inevitably fall to the glacier in case a single misstep was made.

After gaining a point about halfway to the top, I was suddenly brought to a dead stop, with arms outspread, clinging close to the face of the rock, unable to move hand or foot either up or down. My doom appeared fixed. I *must* fall.

When this final danger flashed upon me, I became nerve-shaken for the first time since setting foot on the mountains, and my mind seemed to fill with a stifling smoke. But this terrible eclipse lasted only a moment, when life blazed forth again with preternatural clearness. I seemed suddenly to become possessed of a new sense. The other self, bygone experiences, Instinct, or Guardian Angel—call it what you will—came forward and assumed control. Then my trembling muscles became firm again . . . and my limbs moved with a positiveness and precision with which I seemed to have nothing to do at all. Had I been borne aloft upon wings, my deliverance could not have been more complete. . . . I found a way without effort, and soon stood upon the topmost crag in the blessed light.

THOUSANDS OF TIRED, nerve-shaken, over-civilized people are beginning to find out that going to the mountains is going home; that wildness is a necessity; and that mountain parks and reservations are useful not only as fountains of timber and irrigating rivers, but as fountains of life.

ONLY SPREAD A fern-frond over a man's head and worldly cares are cast out, and freedom and beauty and peace come in.

NATURE IS ALWAYS lovely, invincible, glad, whatever is done and suffered by her creatures. All scars she heals, whether in rocks or water or sky or hearts.

WALK AWAY QUIETLY in any direction and taste the freedom of the mountaineer. Camp out among the grasses and gentians of glacial meadows, in craggy garden nooks full of Nature's darlings. Climb the mountains and get their good tidings. Nature's peace will flow into you as sunshine flows into trees. The winds will blow their own freshness into you, and the storms their energies, while cares will drop off like autumn leaves.

EVENING

he most extravagantly colored of all the sun-
sets I have yet seen in Alaska was one I
enjoyed on the voyage from Portland to
Wrangell. . . . The evening was calm and the sunset colors
came on gradually, increasing in extent and richness of tone
by slow degrees as if requiring more time than usual to
ripen. At a height of about thirty degrees there was a heavy
cloud-bank, deeply reddened on its lower edge and the pro-
jecting parts of its face. Below this were three horizontal
belts of purple edged with gold, while a vividly defined,
spreading fan of flame streamed upward across the purple
bars and faded in a feather edge of dull red. But beautiful
and impressive as was this painting on the sky, the most
novel and exciting effect was in the body of the atmosphere
itself, which, laden with moisture, became one mass of
color—a fine translucent purple haze in which the islands
with softened outlines seemed to float. . . .

WE CAME TO anchor in a beautiful bay, and as the long northern day had still hours of good light to offer, I gladly embraced the opportunity to go ashore to see the rocks and plants. . . . As the twilight began to fall, I sat down on the mossy instep of a spruce. Not a bush or tree was moving; every leaf seemed hushed in brooding repose. One bird, a thrush, embroidered the silence with cheery notes, making the solitude familiar and sweet, while the solemn monotone of the stream sifting through the woods seemed like the very voice of God, humanized, terrestrialized, and entering one's heart as to a home prepared for it. Go where we will, all the world over, we seem to have been there before.

ONE OF THE RICH, ripe days that enlarge one's life—so much of the sun upon one side of it, so much of the moon on the other.

TOWARD SUNSET, ENJOYED a fine run to camp, down the long south slopes, across ridges and ravines, gardens and avalanche gaps, through the firs and chaparral, enjoying wild excitement and excess of strength, and so ends a day that will never end.

EVERY DAY OPENS and closes like a flower, noiseless, effortless. Divine peace glows on all the majestic landscape, like the silent enthusiastic joy that sometimes transfigures a noble human face.

ONE IS CONSTANTLY reminded of the infinite lavishness and fertility of Nature—inexhaustible abundance amid what seems enormous waste. And yet when we look into any of her operations that lie within reach of our minds, we learn that no particle of her material is wasted or worn out. It is eternally flowing from use to use, beauty to yet higher beauty . . . its next appearance will be better and more beautiful than the last.

NOW COMES SUNDOWN. The west is all a glory of color transfiguring everything. Far up the Pilot Peak Ridge the radiant host of trees stand hushed and thoughtful, receiving the Sun's good-night, as solemn and impressive a leave-taking as if sun and trees were to meet no more. The daylight fades, the color spell is broken, and the forest breathes free in the night breeze beneath the stars.

N I G H T

ow the architecture of the forest is seen in all its grandeur. In the daylight we see too much. . . . But at night all is massed, and the spires and towers of black shoot up to the gray sky along the meadow, forming a wall, a street of trees.

WISH I COULD live, like these junipers, on sunshine and snow, and stand beside them on the shore of Lake Tenaya for a thousand years. How much I should see, and how delightful it would be! Everything in the mountains would find me and come to me, and everything from the heavens like light.

LET CHILDREN WALK with Nature, let them see the beautiful blendings and communions of death and life, their joyous inseparable unity, as taught in woods and meadows, plains and mountains and streams of our blessed star, and they will learn that death is stingless indeed, and as beautiful as life.

ONE TOUCH OF nature . . . makes all the world kin.

AFTER SLEEPING a few hours, I stole quietly out of the camp, and climbed the mountain that stands between the two glaciers. The ground was frozen, making the climbing difficult in the steepest places; but the views over [Glacier Bay], sparkling beneath the stars, were enchanting. It seemed then a sad thing that any part of so precious a night had been lost in sleep. The starlight was so full that I distinctly saw not only the berg-filled bay, but most of the lower portions of the glaciers, lying pale and spirit-like amid the mountains. . . . amid so much ice, in the heart of so clear and frosty a night, everything was more or less luminous, and I seemed to be poised in a vast hollow between two skies of almost equal brightness. The exhilarating scramble made me glad and strong and I rejoiced that my studies called me before the glorious night succeeding so glorious a morning had been spent!

SOME OF THE days I have spent alone in the depths of the wilderness have shown me that immortal life beyond the grave is not essential to perfect happiness, for these diverse days were so complete there was no sense of time in them, they had no definite beginning or ending, and formed a kind of terrestrial immortality.

AS LONG AS I live, I'll hear waterfalls and birds and winds sing. I'll interpret the rocks, learn the language of flood, storm, and the avalanche. I'll acquaint myself with the glaciers and wild gardens, and get as near the heart of the world as I can.

MY LEGS SOMETIMES transport me to camp, in the darkness, over cliffs and through bogs and forests that are inaccessible to city legs during the day. In like manner the soul sets forth upon rambles of its own.

EVERYTHING IS flowing—going somewhere, animals and so-called lifeless rocks as well as water. Thus the snow flows fast or slow in grand beauty-making glaciers and avalanches; the air in majestic floods carrying minerals, plant leaves, seeds, spores, with streams of music and fragrance; water streams carrying rocks. . . . While the stars go streaming through space pulsed on and on forever like blood . . . in Nature's warm heart.

I ONLY WENT out for a walk, and finally concluded to stay out till sundown, for going out, I found, was really going in.

THIS GRAND SHOW is eternal. It is always sunrise somewhere; the dew is never all dried at once; a shower is forever falling; vapor is ever rising. Eternal sunrise, eternal sunset, eternal dawn and gloaming, on sea and continents and islands, each in its turn, as the round earth rolls.

A NOTE ON SOURCES

The text selections in this book are drawn from the works of John Muir listed below, followed by the pages on which quotations from each work appear. Ever the conservationist, Muir often recycled his best observations and insights, so that they recur in similar form in more than one source. In such cases, we have referenced the most easily accessible source, rather than necessarily the work (often a periodical) in which the quote first appeared. Page references such as 34a, 34b, are used when two quotations appear on the same page, signifying "top" and "bottom."

Where quotations have been edited, ellipses are conventionally used to represent deleted material, except in a few cases when their proliferation would have been distracting.

Most of the books listed are available in good softcover editions. An excellent reference to Muir's writings, and an extensive collection of quoted material, is Peter Browning's *John Muir: In His Own Words.*

My First Summer in the Sierra (1911): 13, 19a, 21, 23, 31a, 34b, 37, 38, 51, 53a, 58b, 66b, 69, 70, 73b, 80b

The Mountains of California (1894): 14a, 17, 41–42, 46, 54–55

Travels in Alaska (1915): 28, 45, 63, 64, 76

The Yosemite (1912): 24, 27, 33, 83b

John of the Mountains: The Unpublished Journals of John Muir (1938): 8, 14b, 19b, 31b, 42b, 48b, 60, 73a, 75a, 79a

The Story of My Boyhood and Youth (1913): 34a, 75b

Steep Trails (1918): 48a

Our National Parks (1901): 53b, 58a

Overland Monthly (1873): 66a

Autobiographical fragment (undated): 79b

ABOUT THE PHOTOGRAPHER

James Randklev has photographed the American landscape for twenty years, becoming widely recognized for the richness and subtlety of his vision, and his talent for finding vivid patterns amid the quiet details of nature. His intimate knowledge of the natural world was developed as a zoology student at the University of Washington and ranger in Olympic National Park. Photographing primarily with a 4×5 view camera, Randklev has contributed images to leading environmental publications and calendars, including *National Geographic* and *Natural History*. Original prints of his work are represented by private galleries nationwide and in major corporate collections. He currently resides in Tucson, Arizona.

The photographer wishes to dedicate this book:

To the memory of my mother, Eleanor, whose endless love of nature inspired me to capture it on film.

LIST OF PHOTOGRAPHS

The photographs were chosen to complement Muir's words, rather than to illustrate them precisely. All were made within the geographical range of Muir's explorations, and in some cases the image closely depicts what his text describes. Elsewhere, the relationship is more general, as with the Mount Whitney photograph accompanying Muir's adventure on Mount Ritter, or the image simply evokes the mood of the passage.

IN NATURE'S HEART

was designed and produced by Walking Stick
Press, San Francisco, and printed in four-color
process lithography plus varnish by
A. Mondadori, Verona. Scratchboard
illustrations are by David Danz. The text was
composed in Pegasus by Wilsted & Taylor,
Oakland, with display type in Albertus by
Mastertype, San Francisco. The paper is
100 lb. Gardamatt Brillante.